Missing Michael

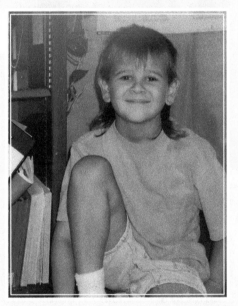

A dad's memory and the things going through my mind.
Watching my son lose the battle against CANCER.

SID HUDGEONS

Fulton Books, Inc.
Meadville, PA

Published by Fulton Books 2020

ISBN 978-1-64654-956-6 (paperback)
ISBN 978-1-64654-957-3 (digital)

Printed in the United States of America

Dedication

I dedicate this book to my son Michael Lynn Hudgeons, and his mom, Sherie Hudgeons.

For his willingness not to give up as long as there was a fight left in his body. He went through so many things, as you will read about here in this book. Please take this book for what it is meant to be: a tribute to him and his fight against cancer.

For I miss him as much today as I did the day he passed away, I just wanted everyone to see firsthand what a terrible thing that CANCER is and what it can do to a person, especially small kids with so much to live for, to be cut short on life so soon without a chance to live and have a family of their own.

I worked a lot, which I will regret that for the rest of my life, while Sherie took care of our son, better than anyone else I could have chosen or paid for. She gave as much as Michael did, in her own way to watch over him the way she did.

I still love my son with all my heart and always will as long as I live. Sherie has a special place in my heart for the things she did; it was her *bone marrow* that gave him a second chance.

We are no longer together, as CANCER, can do harm in more ways than you can imagine.

(The dates at the bottom of each poem are the actual dates that I would be up watching him fight for his life; these things just came to mind as I sit by him.)

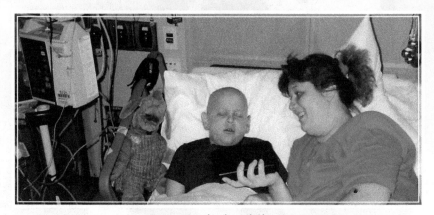

Puppy, Michael, and Sherie

I still remember Michael Lynn
Before that awful day
How he loved to play that ball
That leukemia took away

And now, we sit up late at night
Just to watch him sleep
I remember how my shortstop
Would hustle on his feet

But as the CANCER robbed him
Of bases he could steal
The coaches didn't ponder
They moved him to right field

Mike just couldn't understand
And knew not what to feel
And as they sat him on the bench
Michael Lynn just lost his will

Now, after these three long hard years
Of needles, pills, and such
The radiation has him down
But I love him just as much

His hair is gone; his rash is bad
His skin is peeling fast
But he is still my handsome lad
If he could just sit up and laugh

When he cries out, "Please stop the pain"
My eyes fill up with tears
If he could just be well again
I'd trade GOD all my years

And now, we wait on test results
His pain finally lets him rest
We pray for good news once again
GOD, you put us to the test

And GOD, if you think you need him
Long before his time
I don't have to miss him
I won't be far behind

But if YOU decide to let him stay
And we keep him for our own
I guess the coach I'll have to play
My shortstop's coming home

Love, Dad—1997-11-12

He wakes up every morning
With a smile upon his face
He looks at me and wonders
Will I ever leave this place

His cheeks are round and puffy
From the steroids that he takes
His eyes are red and swollen
From the thirty pills a day

He drinks a bit; he eats a bite
As the doctors make their rounds
I see the hope build in his eyes
But he can't keep food down

His will is strong; his voice is weak
Mike has lost another pound
GOD, how much more can he take
Of meds he can't pronounce

My little man makes me proud
Because he is so brave
I don't know if I could be
With the low survival rate

My little man feels so safe
He just can't wait to play
But a little boy named DJ
Just passed away today

I sit here late night in the dark
I'll be glad when he can leave
Some will never know the joy
Just knowing he still breathes

He felt so bad just yesterday
I walked down a Walmart aisle
Paid twenty for a BB gun
And got a million-dollar smile

Love, Dad—1997-11-15

We have the strongest boy alive
To go through what he goes through
With bone marrow aspirations
And spinal taps by two

With the stitch count on the rise
And his bone marrow on the blink
Another scar, he won't mind
He knows what Mom will think

His mom said, "Son, take some of mine"
"I'll do what I can do"
"You and I will be the same
If this will help you through"

With the platelets and the plasma
And the red cells that they use
He knew he had a second chance
He was getting something new

And even with the Hickman gone
The scar still shows the place
Where another tube had to go
To try to keep him safe

His kidney failed the other day
And another IV strung
It makes me sad to see the scar
Where they had to take his lung

With the PICC line in his right arm
And a fuse-a-port in his chest
They're looking at his jugular vein
To run another test

With the stitch count at two hundred
And one hundred feet of line
We wouldn't take ten million
For our little Frankenstein

Love, Dad—1997-11-30

People let me take you back
To three long years ago
To the night when his screams woke us up
When the bone pain hurt him so

My wife and I jumped out of bed
To see what we could see
We found Michael sitting up
Holding both his knees

"Dad, please stop the bone pain"
Is what we heard him say
I still see his tearstained face
Till this very day

As I picked him up to help
His screams grew loud and deep
As Mom got the heating pad
He yelled, "I can't feel my feet!"

The hours passed like days or years
We feel we've done our best
Mom will have him checked today
But now, he finally rests

Mom called me at half past ten
Her voice was sounding bad
She said the doctors told her
"You need to call his dad"

When I got to the clinic
At straight-up one o'clock
We expected problems
But CANCER was a shock

As I stood over Michael Lynn
While he laid there in this place
As I leaned and kissed his forehead
My TEARS fell upon his face

I looked around to find his mom
Through tears, we tried to see
We asked the lady doctor
"Lord, how could this be?"

We hugged each other, and we cried
But we could not do this long
Michael was a sick little boy
And we had to be strong

We go now to Arnold Palmer
They have to treat him first
We'll never know the pain he's in
It's Michael's HELL on earth

This first day of one thousand
Painful heartsick days
He works so hard, but we still know
GOD could still take him away

Love, Dad—1997-12-02

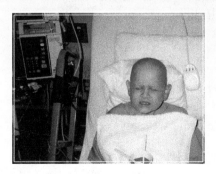

As I woke up this morning
I thought about the past
As the doctors sat and told us
"Michael may not last"

With a tearstained face, we listened
As our hearts just left our souls
He may have about three weeks
The G.V.H. has taken its toll

Michael did have CANCER
His strength is his best tool
Even though he loves it
He's missed two years of school

He tells now of bone pain
As we cry and face the wall
That he had in second grade
Made it hard to walk the halls

He tells of kids that made him cry
"The big kids," he would say
The little ones just stop and stare
At his bald head every day

It's a lack of information
Why his teachers looked like fools
At least they had compassion
He could wear his hat in school

The teachers would not let him play
For fear he would get hurt
While Michael's friends ran and played
He just sat there in the dirt

Now, they talk about a wonder drug
That should be here today
This may give him one more week
It's really hard to say

You've suffered more than anyone
His mom and I have said
"Say any word that comes to mind"
"Scream loud to wake the dead"

Although his anger builds inside
He just smiles that special way
He said, "Mom and Dad, it's alright"
He still doesn't curse today

Love, Dad—1997-12-09

My precious son lies in that room
As he fights to stay alive
His brother came to visit
And sat down by his side

They play games and joke a lot
When Michael has the strength
If me or Mom could take his place
We'd go to any lengths

I fear the end is coming soon
I really hate to say
But if I know Michael Lynn
He's ready for that day

He made a card just for us
He said, "Put it by the tree"
I've learned to hate this time of year
When he said, "Please think of me"

I think he knows the time is near
You can see it in his face
He struggles at night just to breathe
Please let me take his place

We are so proud of our boy
To fight this gallant fight
But there is so much evil here
This just can't be right

Mike just wants to see his room
His dogs and home again
Maybe just to ride his bike
Or play with all his friends

GOD, you speak of men like Noah
And Moses and his friends
That lived at least two hundred years
Why can't Mike have just ten

Love, Dad—1997-12-10

My little man
This to you my pride and joy
You'll never know how proud I am
Of my precious little boy

You give everything you're all and all
If it's work or having fun
From the death bed that you lay on
To that first T-ball home run

You've brought so much joy to us
And you gave us all your trust
It's just so hard for me and Mom
To say when enough's enough

You suffer so much every day
It breaks our heart to see
You'll look up at us one day
And say, "Just leave me be."

I remember just how proud I was
When you made those first few steps
Now, you lay there quietly
I know you've lost your pep

Your few short years here on earth
Has brought us so much joy
I know my heart will break into
If I lose my little boy

Your mom and I have known some pain
But not as much as you
No one on earth I know of
Could go through what you go through

They just told us there is no hope
Then turned and walked away
Your mom and I have broken hearts
We pulled your plug today

Love, Mom and Dad—1997-12-23

We sit and wonder every day
And sometimes half the night
We said, "Go see JESUS"
I hope we told you right

You said that you saw JESUS
You told your mom and me
Of how he talked to you
And things HE let you see

Your mom and I will miss you so
But we know GOD fixed you up
There is no way HE would let
His little angel look so rough

Your little body suffered so
When your organs ceased to work
Your liver quit, your body changed
We knew you really hurt

We miss you all of the time
When we think of the things you did
When I look at your picture
I just have to hang my head

Your mom and I get so upset
That we have to hide our tears
I just can't remember
When I have cried so much in years

We are so lost without you
It worries me sometimes
I just wish there was a way
To turn back the hands of time

I know you are with JESUS
That's what takes up the slack
But I would just give anything
Just to have you back

Now, you've been gone just twenty days
That may not seem so long
I just can hardly stand it
With the thought that you are gone

Love, Dad—1998-01-19

I picked up your batting helmet
Just the other day
My eyes filled up with tears
At the things I tried to say

I hope that we did right by you
With the way we had you done
We have you right here with us
In your precious little urn

We could not stand to see you
In that cold, cold ground somewhere
Like Puppy Killer and Black Jack
We love having you here

Your shrine is so precious
With your trophies, plaques, and such
With your home-run balls and pictures
The things you loved so much

It gives me someplace late at night
To stand and talk to you
While everyone is fast asleep
About the things we used to do

I tried to straighten up your room
The things that you adore
The LEGOs and PlayStation
Your Nintendo 64

I remember how we played those games
Every time my team would fall
You would win by twenty runs
At RBI Baseball

Every time that you would win
I'd act like I was mad
You'd run through the house and yell
"Mom, I've just beat Dad!"

About one out of twenty
Is all that I could win
How I'd just give anything
To lose those games again

We want to keep the things you love
And give some to your friends
We know that's how you'd want it
With your precious life at the end

I just can't stand to get rid of
Anything you ever touched
Your room is full of all your things
We still love you very much

Love, Dad—1998-1-20

I hope you're looking down on us
And see the way we hurt
But please don't feel guilty
Your rest was well deserved

We hurt because we love you
Not because of where you are
We just miss you dearly
You're in a better place by far

I know that you and JESUS
Are having such a blast
For that must be the reason
GOD had you meet HIS SON so fast

Your mom and I now have a way
To speak to you at times
We send up two blue balloons
But our hearts are left behind

We now release a white one
It takes off like the wind
Our eyes fill up with tears
We hope to just see you again

The blue ones are for how we feel
The white one stands for you
Our lives are on hold now
Cause we don't know what to do

The white one always wins the race
Leaves the blue ones far behind
We know you're just the first to leave
That gives us peace of mind

When you're up there helping GOD
And your white balloon goes by
Please take just a moment
When the blue ones pass, say "Hi"

We paint two eyes upon them
So we'll see you once again
For you are not just our son
But also our best friend

Love, Dad—1998-01-27

I had a real bad day today
My mind was playing tricks
I try not to remember
The days you were so sick

I don't want to forget them
Sometimes, it hurts so much
I know how much pain you had
And just how hard you worked

We sit there by your deathbed
We'd make some plans we'd say
I hate we planned our future
When yours would only last one day

I've never seen a CANCER kid
I did not want to hug
They fight so hard to stay alive
It gives my heart a tug

We've seen so many little kids
These three rough years with Mike
Some have died; some lost limbs
And one boy lost his sight

I wonder if the parents
Of the daughters and the sons
Sit up nights and talk to them
The way that we have done

I miss my son so much it hurts
I can't stand to be alone
I just wish there was a way
To bring my Michael home

I know you think about us
I feel it in my guts
I know it must have hurt you too
I know you loved us very much

You used to me tell all the time
"I love you, Dad, so much"
I lay awake a lot at night
Just thinking of your touch

I grounded Michael Lynn one day
Because he broke his truck
He said, "Dad, I don't like you right now"
"But I do love you so much"

Love, Dad—1998-01-28

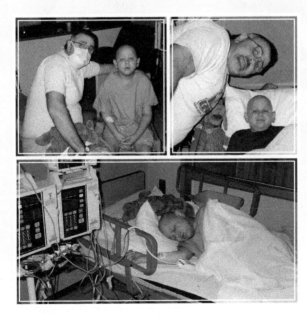

25

I know that you are happy
And feeling oh so great
Not being up there with you
Is what we really hate

Sometimes, we sit and wonder
What makes your mom and I
Have to stay here in this world
And why HE chose you to die

We love you son oh so much
Wish you were by our side
The things we used to laugh about
They now make us cry

We still get cards and phone calls
From people touched by you
Your friends and all the strangers
Loved all the things you do

I really miss my little man
This is like HELL on earth
I guess GOD knew when you would go
I just wish HE'D told us first

We talked about what we would do
After you went away
It hurts not to include you
In the things we plan each day

I think back when you were young
The things you'd want to do
"Son, I just don't want you hurt
Is that too much to ask of you?"

He said, "Dad, just let me be a boy"
About the age of three
"Son, you will fall," I yelled at him
As he climbed up in that tree

If I'd known then, what I know now
When I popped his butt that day
I would have cut off my two hands
And thrown them both away

Love, Dad—1998-01-29

I want to say what I can say
About your last days here
I want to say just how I feel
Between all of my tears

It took one month to do this
Just to build up all my strength
The morning that you passed away
The instant my eyes blinked

The last three months one of us
Was always by your side
Holding on to your small hand
While we watched your body die

Your organs shut down one by one
Your stomach swelled to bust
As we just sat and watched you
Bleed to death in front of us

At least ten bags of blood each day
Went through you way too fast
Your colon bleeding oh so bad
We knew you couldn't last

I just came in and sat back down
From talking with his nurse
His mom was gone, to the store
As our baby left this earth

You were breathing really rough
As I downed my head and cried
  Your breathing stopped, I jumped straight up
It was now six fifty-five

I yelled out loud for some help
"Please check my little guy"
The doctor turned and told me
"Sir, your little man has died"

I put his arms around my neck
To get me one last hug
Then pulled the covers around him
To make sure he was snug

His mom was back from town now
She had picked him up a toy
One look at me, then one at him
She knew we'd lost our pride and joy

As we sit there by his side
And stared into his face
We knew our boy had waited
So we could drive home safe

That long ride home from Gainesville
Without you by our side
The weather still as gloomy
As it had been your last night

It had rained so hard all night
Thanks for taking care of us
And hanging on till morning
You always thought of others first

Love, Dad—1998-01-30

 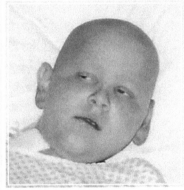

Michael Lynn got mad one day
At everything around
And he took it out on me
As we headed into town

He told me just how picky
I was about my stuff
He told me now "to straighten up"
He said he'd had enough

I snore because I broke my nose
And he had me on tiptoes
And he would not give an inch
He said, "Do something about that nose"

I told him I would work on it
Without turning on a frown
I knew he was not mad at me
But I cried halfway to town

When we got back to the room
Mom had a great big smile
He said he was so sorry
But he would rest now for a while

When he woke up, he was okay
He looked over at Mom
But I was not mad at him
I said, "Son, that is my job"

Anytime he felt like it
He should let off some steam
He knew he had big problems
He deserved to make a scene

I said, "If you can't yell at Dad
When you feel like it, son
Who can you yell at, baby?
I'd be glad to be the one"

Michael had a temper
It would fill up like a cup
If Michael started yelling
You'd better listen up

Love, Dad—1998-01-31

Sometimes when you're sitting there
And think you have it bad
Just read this list I give you
Of the things that Michael had

It's G.V.H. that killed him
And made him look so rough
Three kinds of blood infection
Made it kind of tough

His kidney failed all at once
They put a PICC line in his neck
Two days just before that
They put a Hickman in his chest

They had a smaller PICC line
In his left arm and his right
His fuse-a-port in his side
Made it hard to sleep at night

He had a tube through his nose
His stomach bleeding bad
And when his liver failed
His skin just looked so sad

Another day, his nose bled
It did for seven hours
They could not stop the bleeding
We asked GOD for all his power

With his hair already gone
And now, he's sick at his stomach
His diarrhea turned to blood
And now, he'd start to vomit

He had been in bed so long
His feet just had no feeling
Every time they'd move the tape
His skin would just start peeling

This went on for five straight days
But right in there he hung
Oh, I forgot to mention
They already took one lung

Now, they say the lining's gone
In his GI tract and colon
He knew he would lose the fight
With his stomach really swollen

My son died a painful death
Had pain you can't imagine
But in my eyes, he looked so good
He could win a beauty pageant

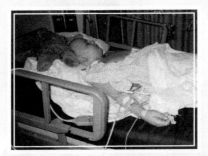

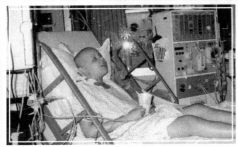

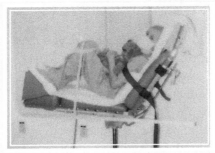

Full-Body Radiation

Love, Dad—1998-02-07

Michael and I talked one night
The idea came up again
"No one would trade their place with me
Cause of the pain I'm in"

I will trade with you, my son
I told you time again
His smile grew wide; I was so proud
I'll take the pain you're in

Son, I'll take your place right now
I'll trade with you today
He smiled as if to test me
"I know, Dad. You tell me every day"

I think about your last few days
When you were so out of it
The morphine had you sleepy
Your mind wanted to quit

You were passing so much blood
I had to lift you up
And help to change your bed
You relied on me so much

You were in bed so long
Your skin was really bad
From sleeping on your back
I know the tough time that you had

We kept his ole stuffed puppy
Right next to his side
When he was not unconscious
He would kiss that dog goodnight

You did not deserve the pain
As a son, you were the best
Son, we wanted you to live
Not die that terrible death

Love, Dad—1991-02-08

He asked me once with tearstained eyes,
"Dad, why did I get CANCER?"
This is your biggest question yet
"Son, I don't have that answer"

We don't know why HE chose you
I guess 'cause you're so strong
HE saw the way you worked so hard
And you never proved HIM wrong

I know just how sick you were
Those days you tried to dose
Your hands and arms were so weak
You let me scratch your nose

I asked you if that felt alright
And you'd nod your head to say
"Yes, Dad, that hits the spot
Don't take your hand away"

We talked to you a lot, son
We hoped you heard us too
You got to where you could not see
We knew we were losing you

We used to ask you questions
While you lay there in your bed
Things that you could answer
With a short nod of your head

Like "Son, you know we love you?'
And "Do you feel good today?"
And "Did JESUS come to see you?"
"You know HE'LL show you the way

You cannot talk; you can't sit up
You've been silent now for days
Now, the morphine keeps you quiet
While your life just slips away

The morphine keeps you out of pain
While you rest a while today
We listen now to tapes you made
Of the things you used to say

It seems like ten years ago
When I bought that thing for you
You put on tape your Christmas list
And things you'd like to do

You said you needed a new bat
When Christmas felt the same
Then asked GOD through bleeding lips
Not to be in so much pain

You said to get this over with
And take care of everyone
Don't make me sleep in hospital beds
When everything is done

It just didn't seem like Christmas
As we watched you feel so bad
I can't believe we sit here now
You gave everything you had

You said JESUS would be back
To get you that's for sure
HE said, "How you doing, Mike?"
HE knew he had your cure

Love, Dad—1998-02-24

Michael Lynn

Bat Michael

Mom and I miss him so
It's your choice we would say
You can go live with JESUS
Unless it's here you want to stay

JESUS said, "You have a choice"
To a brave boy such as you
That's what you told us HE had said
Mike, do what's best for you

If you have a choice, son
I know what it will be
To fly around on all those clouds
Not be sick with Mom and me

One-third of your life here
Was just pain and hurt and such
If you decide to go with HIM
We'll miss you very much

Your life down here was awful
You suffered really bad
If you leave, you won't miss
The awful time you had

If you go live with JESUS
Or you stay with us
HE will make you well again
Just give HIM all your trust

No matter where you go, son
Your things are still right here
When JESUS lets you check us out
You'll know that we still care

We have a place for all your stuff
It's right next to my bed
When I really need to see you
I just have to raise my head

Love, Dad—1998-03-16

Put yourself in Mike's shoes
I'll give you his same test
The one that JESUS gave him
Just before he went to rest

"Do you want to fly with ME
And have a million friends for play?"
"Or be real sick and vomit
For sixty-five straight days?"

"Do you want to feel real good
And help some friends in need?"
"Or just lay there in ICU
And hurt and sleep and bleed?"

"Let's go have some fun, Mike
I know some things to do"
"Or just lay there and lose your lung
That's what's in store for you?"

"Mike, do you want to lay there
That Hickman really stings?"
"Let's just fly up to cloud nine
And hear some angels sing"

To me, those PICC lines were the worst
A wire throughout your veins
Michael Lynn didn't hang around
Go, hear those angels sing

They ran a scope up his butt
How degrading that must be
"Do you want that done again
Or come go play with ME?"

They did everything they could
The test, the lines, the pain
"Come go with ME, my little man
I'll make you well again"

JESUS gave him every choice
All the ups and all the downs
Michael Lynn has made it clear
He wants to leave this town

Gainesville, he is out of here
But not by truck or car
Michael is not sick no more
He's in a better place by far

Mom and I can read his mind
We've watched him really hurt
We know just what he will say
"You can have this place called Earth"

Love, Dad—1998-03-16

Michael and his   Michael's Brother Matt
brother Rick

I look up in the sky now
And see the clouds above
I wonder where my Michael is
And send him all my love

I went to see a movie
Late this afternoon
I got upset at one part
I hope to see you soon

They had this little boy strapped down
In his hospital bed
It brought those old memories
Of some things that you said

The nurses had you strapped down
In your ICU bed
My heart just broke again
As my mind heard what you said

You said, "Unbuckle me"
With your soft voice almost gone.
I said, "You're not buckled up"
"Your nurses have gone home"

They had him strapped for his own good
'Cause he tried to leave one time
We had to leave on shift change
He was trying to lose his mind

I helped to roll you on your side
As I help to change your bed
You asked, "Dad, can we just go home?"
Through your tears, that's what you said

"Baby boy, I wish we could"
As I cleaned your bloody bed
JESUS, please, just look at him
Let him live and me be dead

Love, Dad—1998-03-17

Today is your birthday
Mike, we miss you so
You made us very happy
Ten short years ago

I remember very well
When they said, "Here is your son"
I told his mom, "I love you so"
For the good deed she had done

His first birthday we had a tape
He was barely walking round
Mom and I now sit real quiet
Just listening for his sound

His second party was okay
His nanny was there then
He had his friends; he laughed a lot
We wish just to see him again

Then, there was his third birthday
If I am thinking right
We removed his training wheels
He had learned to ride his bike

Now, we've counted up to four
Proud parents that we are
Another birthday party
From him we don't get far

Your fifth birthday is here at last
"Come on," we both would call
"Don't forget your glove and bat"
It was time to play T-ball

His sixth was here; he's still with us
We laugh hard to bust a stitch
I've never seen a bigger smile
When they let him play coach-pitch

Now, we're up to seven
Just before the CANCER strikes
Two months later, he'd be up
With his knee pain half the night

Eight years old and going strong
The chemo was helping fast
But we could see his body fade
We hoped these days would last

Nine years old, his party grand
Most kids he'd ever had
Yes, Yoda and Darth Vader
By the space walk, oh so bad

The kids told everyone at school
The best party, so to speak
But we did not know his relapse
Would be here in twelve weeks

Ten is here; our hearts are broken
Our son is here no more
We cry so much we miss him so
Our hearts are really sore

It's time now for home movies
His tapes we'll listen to
We'll look at pictures of our boy
Michael Lynn, we both love you

Love, Dad—1998-04-22

Happy birthday, son

I think about the day we left
The morning that you died
My tears running down your cheek
As I hugged your neck goodbye

I put one arm around me
Your left one, not your right
They had too many needles there
'Cause it hurt you every night

We told you that we loved you
And you were going for a ride
Your best nurse and her two friends
Would be right by your side

We are so sorry baby
I feel that we have lied
When we said, "You would get well"
We never thought that you would die

Michael Lynn, you suffered so
As the life went from your eyes
We pulled your plug; there was no hope
While we sit there by your side

Once we stopped all the machines
And your clock was running down
We knew you were going fast
Your doctors ceased to come around

You hung in there for three short days
And three long sleepless nights
You would show them one last time
Michael Lynn knew how to fight

Yes, we love you, Michael Lynn
And we are proud of you
We will miss the man you are
And the little boy in you

Love, Dad—1998-04-23

I'm sitting here; it's late again
I cried a lot today
I really just don't understand
Why you had to go away

I really miss you, little man
The sadness just gets worst
I need to see your face again
I just can't stand the hurt

I think of doing something bad
To get to be with you
I don't like it down here too much
I just need to be with you

I know a way to leave here soon
If it's alright with you
I know how to end the pain
Will you forgive me if I do

I'm pretty much used up now
Worthless, if you will
I need to know if it's okay
To come meet you on the hill

JESUS needs to say okay
But on the other hand
He used up the perfect boy
When HE took my little man

I may just see you real soon
I may not wait for HIS okay
I've got to kiss that face again
Well, son, what do you say?

Love, Dad—1999-12-10

Happy birthday, Michael Lynn
My son that had to go
Sixteen years you would have been
If CANCER hadn't hurt you so

It's April twenty-second
A day I won't forget
GOD has needed you I guess
But my eyes are very wet

It really seems a long time now
And sometimes like yesterday
It's been seven years now
Since we sat and watched you play

So many things you never did
Or got to see, or say
I hope you're happy there with GOD
We still miss you today

Love, Dad—2000-04-22

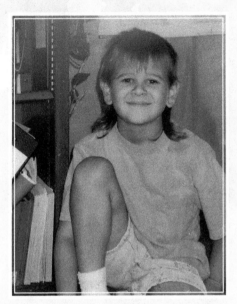

Michael Lynn Hudgeons
Born 1988-04-22
Died 1997-12-23

I have never been so sad
In all my fifty years
As each time when I think
That you're no longer here

Eleven years you'd be this month
On that twenty-second day
My heart still breaks every time
I wonder why you went away

Everyone says GOD knows best
When HE takes these kids that way
I will never really understand
Until my dying day

Little Michael suffered so
From the things that CANCER did
He saw too many painful days
For just a little kid

He had the strength of forty men
To go through what he did then
Not to complain of where he'd been
That was my Michael Lynn

I've prayed for that day to come
To trade places with my boy
But GOD would not take me
But he took my little boy

Love, Dad—1998-04-19

I just woke up feeling sad
It's Father's Day today
And it's really not the same
Since my baby went away

It used to be a special day
With my little man around
He would get a card for me
He and Mom would run to town

He got a special card for me
For no one else but you
He'd record his little voice
For me to listen to

He sang a song just for me
The way he used to do
He sang, "Happy Father's Day
Happy Father's Day to you"

Then, his little mind went blank
To the card he was to send
Then, he sang, "I love you
I love you, Dad, the end"

I played that card ten times today
As I sat there with my fears
With every word he sang to me
I cried one hundred tears

He's been gone six months now
And there is no end in sight
The pain gets worst every day
And doubles every night

Love, Dad—1998-06-21

Mom and I are sad right now
You've been gone nine months today
We miss "Good morning, Mom and Dad"
That's what you used to say

We talked about how lonesome
On that last elevator ride
When they took you from your room
The morning that you died

You had to go downstairs
To the basement underground
They say that's where you have to go
When your spirit's not around

We worried just how lonely
On that last ride you might be
We had never thought about
One more ride we failed to see

After we planned your funeral
Through tears, we heard him say
"I know you'll want him home real soon"
"I'll go get Mike myself today"

I thought about that trip today
That last long trip he's on
All by himself in the back
My baby's coming home

Love, Dad—1998-09-23

I passed by a store today
One I said that we'd go in
I put you off so many times
And it breaks my heart again

I did not have time for you
But I did not know that then
I thought that work should come first
And it breaks my heart again

You'd say, "Dad, let's go see that"
"But can't we just go in?"
"Maybe next time, little man"
And it breaks my heart again

The Dinosaur Store on the beach
"But, Dad, it's only ten"
"Michael Lynn, I don't have time"
And it breaks my heart again

"But, Dad I won't buy anything"
"Just look at that caveman"
"Son, I have to get to work"
And it breaks my heart again

I put you off so many times
Now, all I have is time on hand
Michael Lynn, how many times
Did I BREAK YOUR HEART again?

Love, Dad—1999-12-10

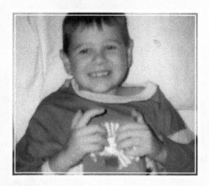

You've been gone six months now
One hundred eighty days
I think of you each hour
And every minute of the day

We have your pictures everywhere
On the icebox at the house
In the car and on the walls
And by your giant Mickey Mouse

Every time we turn our heads
Your smiling face we see
I run and hug your pictures
And get that special kiss for me

Mom does the same thing
We see those pretty eyes
We laugh and say we love you
Then both sit down and cry

We are so glad you're safe now
Without the pain at last
We saw you worked so hard
But that CANCER worked so fast

We both love you so much
Just say hi to us at night
When you see us in our dreams
Have fun and just sleep tight

Love, Dad—1998-06-23

Eighteen years ago today
I kissed your little face
I'm sorry that you hurt so much
No one still can take your place

I try to think about how you would look
I know you would be tall
Mom and I were happy then
We thought we had it all

I hope these eighteen years with GOD
You have been happy too
Mom and I have had rough times
But you know we both love you

We dream about you all the time
And we talk about you so
But we still don't understand
Why HE chose you to go

It wasn't fair; you were so young
And such a handsome face
You know that either one of us
Would gladly take your place

Love, Dad—2006-02-22

I fed your ole dog Black Jack
The one you needed so
When your fever was so high
You got when they let you go

I wish I would have let you run
And play games of all sort
I was so scared you would hit
Your left-side fuse-a-port

I guess I worried way too much
About simple things like that
You and she were having fun
Son, I take back all of that

If you were just half as proud
Of me as I am of you
I would be a happy man
I can't do the things you do

I wish I were up there real high
On a cloud built just for two
I feel so close to you each night
In the dreams I have of you

Thanks for the hugs and kisses
You give me late at night
I dreamed you said, "I feel really good"
Although it didn't seem right

I asked if you were happy there
In heaven way up high
I don't think they'll let you say
You just smiled and waved bye-bye

Come and visit anytime
Come see me any night
I'll take those hugs and kisses
I won't put up a fight

Love, Dad—1998-04-01

The many faces of Michael
The ones that we miss so
That happy smile of yours
Said I'll never let you go

There was one you did not need
With that deep frown we would know
We saw this one more and more
When the CANCER hurt you so

That happy laugh would light you up
With your face glowing bright
We saw this one last awhile
Before that CANCER won its fight

We saw the face of question
In that hospital at night
After your bone marrow
Stopped putting up a fight

The face after your transplant
The wide grin for us to see
We think you knew it would not work
It was just for Mom and me

Every picture that we have
Shows another side of you
The faces of our little boy
So big, so bright, so true

Love, Dad—1998-08-14

I listen to your voice sometimes
On the tapes you made one night
While we sit up there at Shands
In vain, you fought your fight

If we had known the ending
More tapes we would have had
You were so sweet you always said
"I love you, Mom and Dad"

You were so sweet we love you so
You're still our pride and joy
JESUS knows HE has the best
We just miss our little boy

I wish you were still here with me
As you opened your new toy
I know Mom had spent a bunch
On a special little boy

You would get more toys each year
Than I'd had all my life
She has been a special mom
And a very special wife

I know you miss your mother
Your love you never hid
You know that she loved you too
By the special things she did

I'll just say goodbye, son
And throw a kiss good night
Just hug me close in my dreams
That's worth all the toys in sight

Love, Dad—1998-07-04

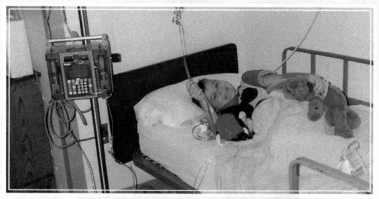

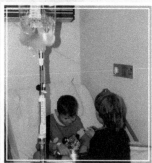

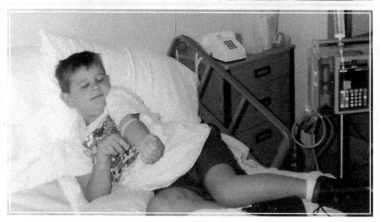

Michael's mom

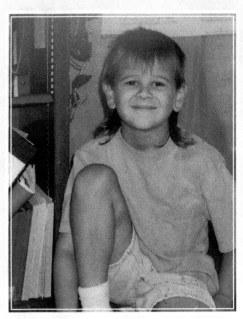

This is how Michael Lynn started out with leukemia.

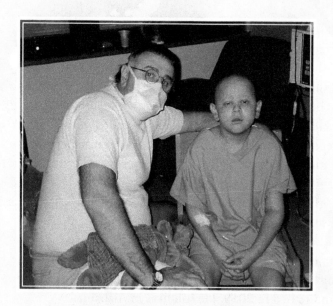

This is what CANCER can do to a perfect little boy. Please take this book and pictures the right way. I mean only GREAT RESPECT for my son and what CANCER does to children. I just wanted all to see how my son and all kids fight just to try to see another day. I miss him every day...Love, Dad.

About the Author

Sid Hudgeons grew up in Texas and lived in a small town. About the age of fourteen (about 1964), he went to live on a ranch with his father and stepmother; his parents were divorced when they were younger. He, his little brother, and his cousin would take turns driving the jeep and chasing the bulls through the pasture and jumping on them and try to ride them. He lived there until his father was killed in a car wreck in 1971 (his stepmother had died one year earlier); then, he willed the ranch to two kids of a friend of his. After that, Sid worked in the oil fields of Texas and Wyoming until the 1980s. In the 1970s, he married and had a son, Matt. In the 1980s, he married, and Michael was born. After Michael died, he and his wife split up and went their separate ways. He worked in management in the roofing industry for three different companies for thirty years. He moved to Alabama in 2017 and finished working for the last company; he likes Alabama, so he decided to stay there and retired in 2019. He still lives in Alabama.